ADORN

BY KNIT PICKS

Printed in the United States of America

First Printing, 2015

ISBN 978-1-62767-096-8

Versa Press, Inc
800-447-7829

www.versapress.com

CONTENTS

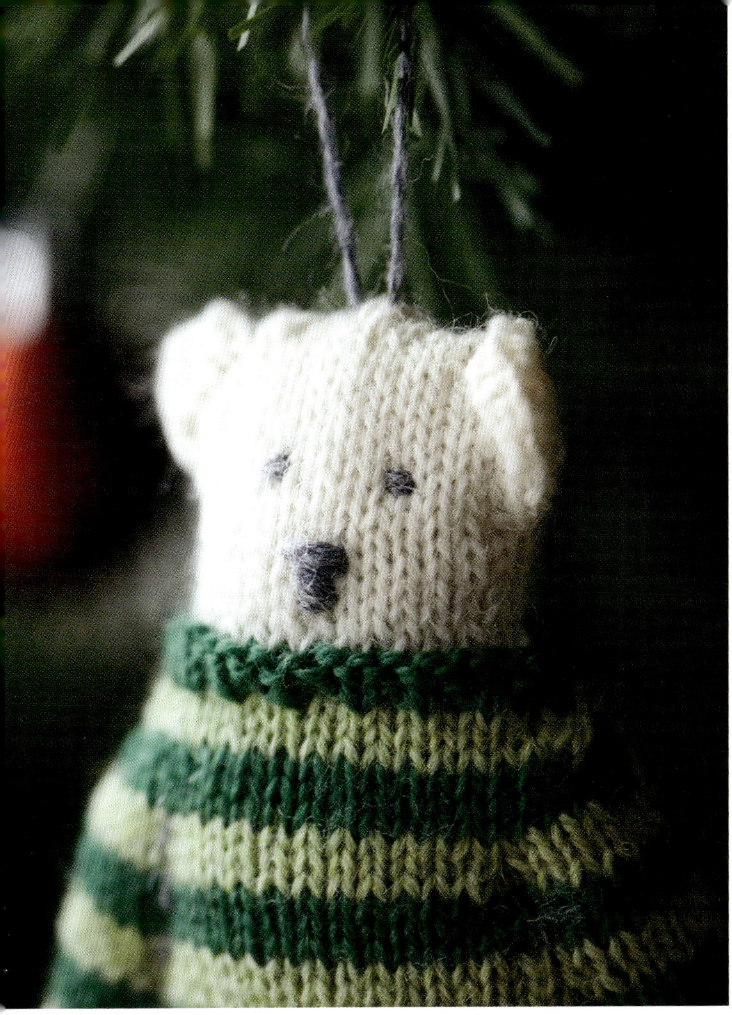

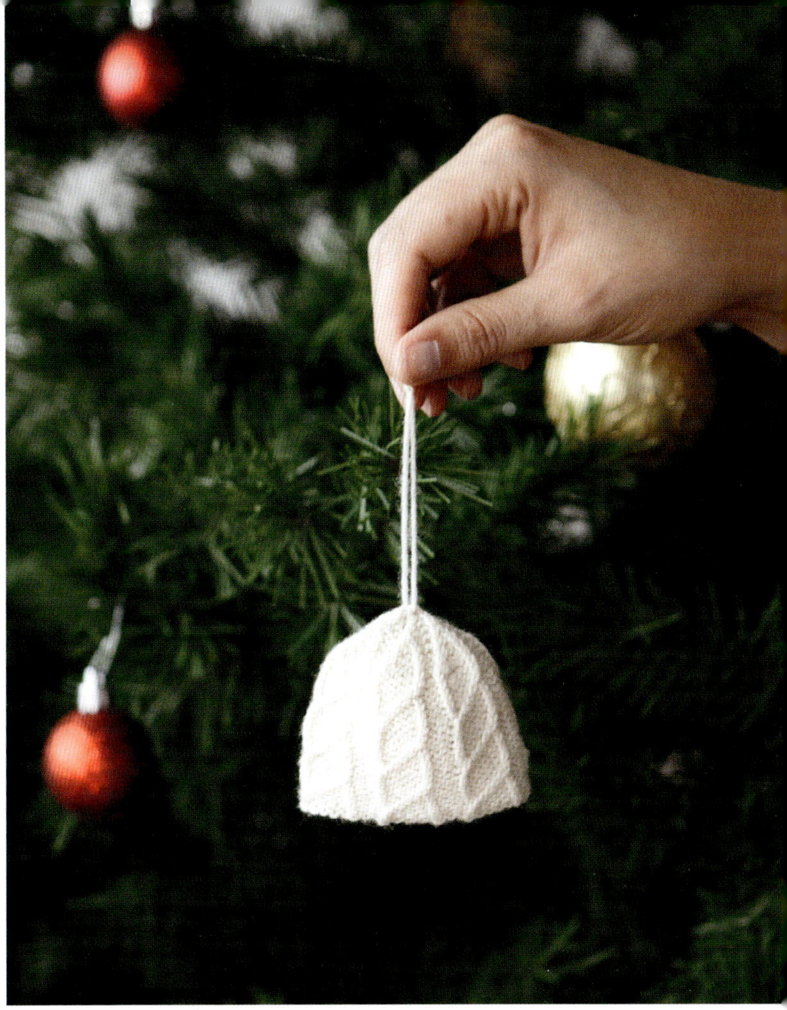

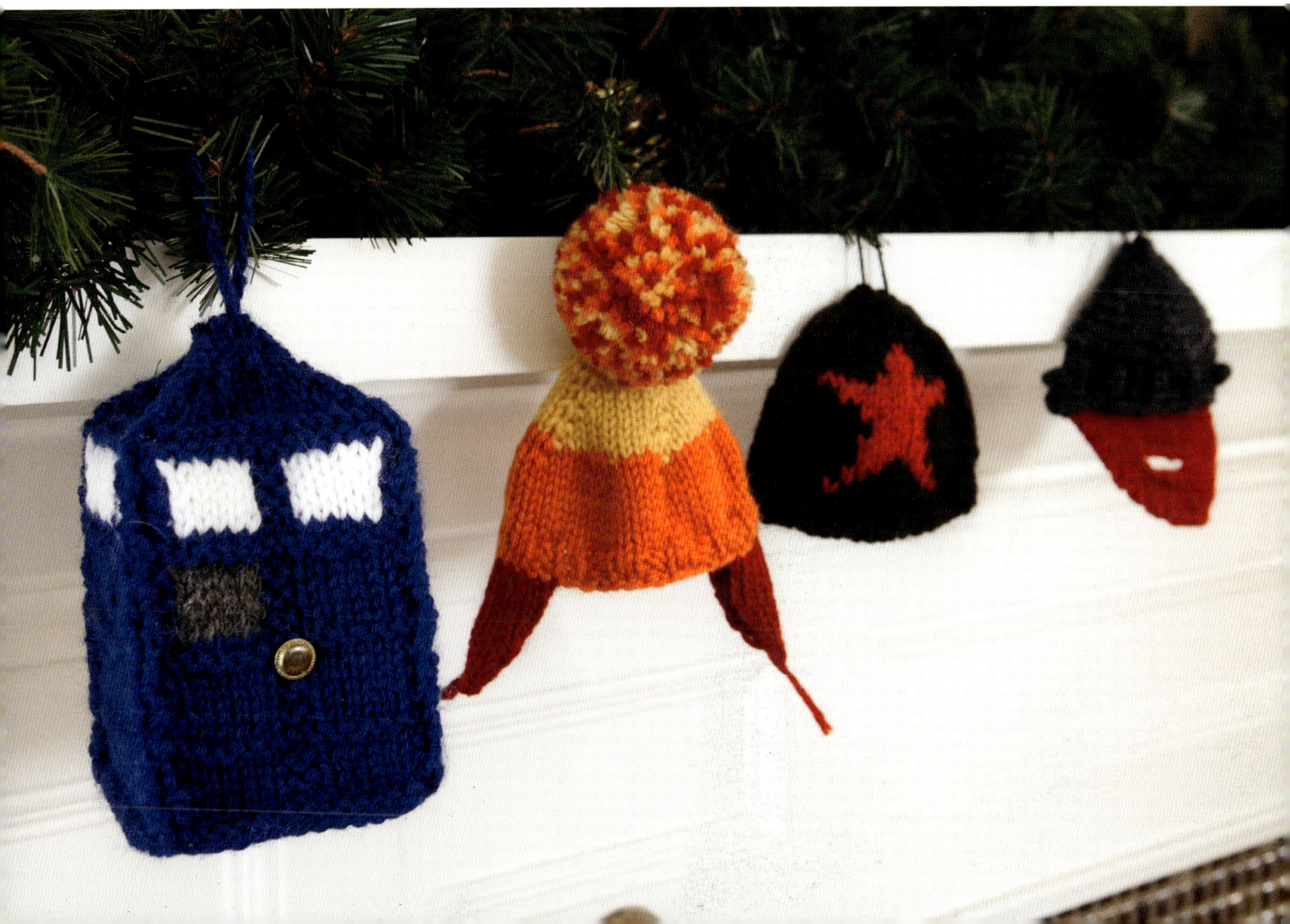

ARCTIC ATTIRE

by Annie Watts

FINISHED MEASUREMENTS

Socked Snowshoe Hare: 2.5" wide x 6.5" high
Walrus: 6.5" wide x 3.75" high
Whale: 6.5" wide x 3" high
Polar Bear: 3.25" wide x 5.25" high

YARN

Knit Picks Palette (100% Peruvian Highland Wool; 231 yards/50g):
Macaw 25530; Cream 23730; Marble Heather 24244; Briar Heather 26058; Serrano 24553; Oregon Coast Heather 25541; Asphalt Heather 24243; Pimento 24246; Grass 24585; Green Tea Heather 24258

NEEDLES

US 2 (3mm) DPNs or two 24" circular needles for two circulars technique, or one 32" or longer circular needle for Magic Loop technique, or size to obtain gauge
US 5 (3.75mm) DPNs, or three sizes larger than size to obtain gauge (for portions of Walrus and Whale)

NOTIONS

Yarn Needle
Stitch Markers
Fiberfill
Scrap Yarn or Stitch Holder (for Whale)

GAUGE

32 sts and 44 Rnds = 4" over St st in the round on smaller needles, blocked

Arctic Attire

Notes:

These arctic animals are all ready for winter! Their stylish accessories add a whimsical touch to these adorable ornaments. Choose from the cheerful Walrus, graceful Whale, skipping Snowshoe Hare or the rotund Polar Bear. They'll help you decorate in arctic style this year!

Wrap & Turn (W&T)

Work until the stitch to be wrapped. Bring yarn to the front of the work, slip next st as if to purl, return the yarn to the back; turn work and slip wrapped st onto RH needle. Continue across row. Picking up wraps: Work to the wrapped st. Insert the RH needle under the wrap(s), then through the wrapped st Kwise. Knit the wrap(s) together with the wrapped st.

3-Needle Bind Off

* Hold the two pieces of knitting together with the points facing to the right. Insert a third needle into the first st on each of the needles Kwise, starting with the front needle. Work a knit st, pulling the loop through both of the sts you've inserted the third needle through. After pulling the loop through, sl the first st off of each of the needles. Repeat from *. Pass the first finished st over the second and off of the needle.

Kitchener Stitch (grafting)

With an equal number of sts on two needles, hold needles parallel, with WS's facing in and both needles pointing to the right. Perform Step 2 on the first front st, and then Step 4 on the first back st, and then continue with instructions below.
1: Pull yarn needle Kwise through front st and drop st from knitting needle.
2: Pull yarn needle Pwise through next front st, leave st on knitting needle.
3: Pull yarn needle Pwise through first back st and drop st from knitting needle.
4: Pull yarn needle Kwise through next back st, leave st on knitting needle.
Repeat steps 1 – 4 until all sts have been grafted.

SOCKED SNOWSHOE HARE

Yarn

A Macaw 25530; B Cream 23730; C Marble Heather 24244; one skein each

Notes:

The ornament is meant to look two-dimensional. To achieve this effect, stuff only lightly. Stitching around the arms after stuffing will pucker the body to look like arms. Arm stitching will run along the increase and decrease line between Rnd 9 and Rnd 20. See photos.

Directions

Socks (make two)

With Color A and smaller needles (used for all sections of the Hare), CO 6 sts. Join to work in the round, PM if desired.
Rnd 1: (K1, KFB, K1) twice. (8 sts)
Rnds 2-11: Knit.
Stuff the foot of the sock here.

Rnd 12 (heel): K7, W&T; P6, W&T; K5, W&T; P4, W&T; K3, W&T; P2, W&T; K2, W&T; P2, W&T; K3, W&T; P4, W&T; K5, W&T; P6, W&T; K7.
Rnds 13-18: Knit.
Rnd 19: (K1, P1, KFB) twice, K1, P1. (10 sts)
Rnds 20-25: (K1, P1) to end.
Bind off loosely in pattern. Break yarn, leaving a 6" tail.

Place your pinky or a large gauge knitting needle inside the sock. Fold the ribbed part of the sock down, exposing the WS purl ridges of the last knit Rnd. Using the tail, stitch the edge of the cuff to the outside of a sock a couple of times so it stays in place. Stuff the rest of the sock.

Body

Take the first sock and one DPN. With the sock toe facing right, PU 4 sts across the top, through the purl loops from the last knit Rnd. On the same needle, do the same with the second sock. With a second DPN, PU 4 sts on the left side of the second sock, with a third DPN, PU 4 sts on the left side of the first sock. The beginning of the rnd will be on the toe-side of these needles. 16 sts.

Rnd 1: With Color B, CO 1, K4 from first sock, K4 from second sock, CO 2, K4 from second sock, K4 from first sock, CO 1. (20 sts)
Rnd 2: (KFB, K8, KFB) twice. (24 sts)
Rnd 3: (KFB, K10, KFB) twice. (28 sts)
Rnd 4: (KFB, K12, KFB) twice. (32 sts)
Rnd 5: Knit.
Rnd 6: (KFB, K14, KFB) twice. (36 sts)
Rnds 7-8: Knit.
Rnd 9: KFB, K15, K2tog, SSK, K15, KFB.
Rnd 10: KFB, K1, KFB, K30, KFB, K1, KFB. (40 sts)
Rnd 11: KFB, K2, KFB, K32, KFB, K2, KFB. (44 sts)
Rnd 12: KFB, K3, KFB, K34, KFB, K3, KFB. (48 sts)
Rnd 13: Knit.
Rnd 14: Knit.
Rnd 15: K22, SSK, K2tog, K22. (46 sts)
Rnd 16: Knit.
Rnd 17: K2tog, K42, SSK. (44 sts)
Rnd 18: K2tog, K18, SSK, K2tog, K18, SSK. (40 sts)
Rnd 19: K2tog, K36, SSK. (38 sts)
Rnd 20: K2tog, K34, SSK. (36 sts)
Rnd 21: K16, SSK, K2tog, K16. (34 sts)
Rnds 22-23: Knit.
Rnd 24: K2tog, K13, SSK, K2tog, K13, SSK. (30 sts)
Rnd 25: Knit.
Rnd 26: K2tog, K26, SSK. (28 sts)
Rnd 27: K12, SSK, K2tog, K12. (26 sts)
Rnd 28: K2tog, K22, SSK. (24 sts)
Rnd 29: K2tog, K20, SSK. (22 sts)
Rnd 30: K9, SSK, K2tog, K9. (20 sts)
Stuff the body here.

Head

Rnd 31: KFB, K18, KFB. (22 sts)
Rnd 32: KFB, K20, KFB. (24 sts)
Rnd 33: Knit.
Rnd 34: KFB, K22, KFB. (26 sts)

Rnd 35: KFB, K24, KFB. (28 sts)
Rnd 36: Knit.
Rnd 37: KFB, K26, KFB. (30 sts)
Rnd 38: KFB, K28, KFB. (32 sts)
Rnd 39: Knit.
Rnd 40: K2tog, K28, SSK. (30 sts)
Rnd 41: K2tog, K26, SSK. (28 sts)
Rnd 42: Knit.
Rnd 43: (K2tog, K10, SSK) twice. (24 sts)
Rnd 44: (K2tog, K8, SSK) twice. (20 sts)
Rnd 45: (K2tog, K6, SSK) twice. (16 sts)
Rnd 46: (K2tog, K4, SSK) twice. (12 sts)
Rnd 47: (K2tog, K2, SSK) twice. (8 sts)

Stuff the head.
Break yarn. Graft the front and back sts together using kitchener stitch.

Ears (make two)
With Color B, CO 4 sts. Join to work in the round, PM if desired.
Rnd 1: Knit.
Rnd 2: (KFB, K1) twice. (6 sts)
Rnd 3: Knit.
Rnd 4: (K1, KFB, K1) twice. (8 sts)
Rnds 5-6: Knit.
Rnd 7: (K1, KFB, K2) twice. (10 sts)
Rnds 8-10: Knit.
Rnd 11: (K2, KFB, K2) twice. (12 sts)
Rnds 12-16: Knit.

Work a Three-Needle Bind Off. Break yarn, leaving a 6" tail for seaming.

Tail
With Color B, CO 1 st. Leave a short but usable tail.
Row 1 (RS): *K into the front of the stitch, keeping the stitch on the left needle, K into the back of the stitch, keeping the stitch on the left needle repeat from *; K into the front of the stitch once more. (increase one st to five). (5 sts)
Row 2: KFB, K1, KFB, K1, KFB. (8 sts)
Row 3: Knit.
Row 4: Purl.
Rows 5-6: Rep Rows 3-4.
Row 7: K2tog, K1, K2tog, K1, K2tog. (5 sts)
Row 8: P3tog, P2tog, pass first st over the second. (1 st)

Break yarn leaving a short tail, pull through last st.

Finishing
Weave in ends.
Fold bottom edge of each ear in half. Stitch the ears on either side of the head as shown. Stitch the cast on and bind off yarn tails of the Tail together, making a small ball. Stitch to the body as shown.

Using Color C stitch eyes and nose as shown. Stitch around the front to form the paws along the increase and decrease line between Rnd 9 and Rnd 20 as shown.

Thread 5" of yarn or ribbon through top, tie together to hang ornament from.

WALRUS
Yarn
A Briar Heather 26058; B Serrano 24553; C Cream 23730; D Oregon Coast Heather 25541; E Asphalt Heather 24243; one skein each

Notes:
The ornament is meant to look two-dimensional. To achieve this effect, stuff only lightly. Three different colors are used to stitch the face, see photos for reference.

Directions
Head
With Color A and smaller needles (used for all sections of the Walrus except the Hat), CO 8 sts leaving a long tail to close up the top later. Join to work in round, PM if desired.
Rnd 1: (KFB, K2, KFB) twice. (12 sts)
Rnd 2: Knit.
Rnd 3: (KFB, K4, KFB) twice. (16 sts)
Rnd 4: Knit.
Rnd 5: (KFB, K6, KFB) twice. (20 sts)
Rnd 6: Knit.
Rnd 7: (KFB, K8, KFB) twice. (24 sts)
Rnd 8: Knit.
Rnd 9: (KFB, K10, KFB) twice. (28 sts)
Rnds 10-12: Knit.
Rnd 13: (KFB, K12, KFB) twice. (32 sts)
Rnd 14: Knit.

Body
Rnd 15: K15, KFB, KFB, K15. (34 sts)
Rnd 16: (KFB, K15, KFB) twice. (38 sts)
Rnd 17: K18, KFB, KFB, K18. (40 sts)
Rnd 18: K19, KFB, KFB, K19. (42 sts)
Rnd 19: K20, KFB, KFB, K20. (44 sts)
Rnd 20: K21, KFB, KFB, K21. (46 sts)
Rnd 21: K22, KFB, KFB, K22. (48 sts)
Rnd 22: K23, KFB, KFB, K23. (50 sts)
Rnd 23: K24, KFB, KFB, K24. (52 sts)
Rnd 24: K25, KFB, KFB, K25. (54 sts)
Rnd 25: K26, KFB, KFB, K26. (56 sts)
Rnd 26: K27, KFB, KFB, K27. (58 sts)
Rnd 27: K28, KFB, KFB, K28. (60 sts)
Rnd 28: K29, KFB, KFB, K29. (62 sts)
Rnd 29: K30, KFB, KFB, K30. (64 sts)
Rnd 30: K31, KFB, KFB, K31. (66 sts)
Rnd 31: K32, KFB, KFB, K32. (68 sts)
Rnd 32: K33, KFB, KFB, K33. (70 sts)
Rnd 33: K34, KFB, KFB, K34. (72 sts)
Rnd 34: SSK, K33, KFB, KFB, K33, K2tog.
Rnd 35: K35, KFB, KFB, K35. (74 sts)
Rnd 36: SSK, K34, KFB, KFB, K34, K2tog.
Rnd 37: Same as Rnd 36.

Bottom Edge
Break yarn, leaving 18" tail. Kitchener together the last 25 sts of the round with the first 25 sts of the round. 24 sts remain. Stuff body here.

Tail

Rejoin Color A. Knit 12, place remaining 12 sts on scrap yarn.

*CO 12 sts, join to work in the round. (24 sts)

Rnd 1: Knit.

Rnd 2: (SSK, K8, K2tog) twice. (20 sts)

Rnd 3: Knit.

Rnd 4: (SSK, K6, K2tog) twice. (16 sts)

Rnd 5: Knit.

Rnd 6: (SSK, K4, K2tog) twice. (12 sts)

Rnds 7-10: Knit.

Rnd 11: (SSK, K2, K2tog) twice. (8 sts)

Rnds 12-15: Knit.

Rnd 16: (K1, K2tog, K1) twice. (6 sts)

Rnds 17-18: Knit.

Rnd 19: K3tog twice. (2 sts)

Break yarn leaving an 8" tail, pull through remaining sts.

Place 12 held sts back on needles, repeat from * to form the other half of the tail.

Flippers (make two)

With Color A, CO 6 sts. Join to work in the round, PM if desired.

Rnd 1: Knit.

Rnd 2: KFB, K4, KFB. (8 sts)

Rnds 3-4: Knit.

Rnd 5: KFB, K6, KFB. (10 sts)

Rnds 6-10: Knit.

Rnd 11: K9, turn; Sl 1, P7, turn; Sl 1, K6, turn; Sl 1, P5, turn; Sl 1, K7.

Rnd 12: Knit.

Rnd 13: KFB, K8, KFB. (12 sts)

Rnd 14: Knit.

Rnd 15: KFB, K10, KFB. (14 sts)

Rnd 16: Knit.

Rnd 17: KFB, K12, KFB. (16 sts)

Rnd 18: Knit.

Work a 3-Needle Bind Off. Break yarn, leaving an 8" tail.

Hat

With Color B, CO 24 sts. Join to work in the round, PM if desired.

Rnds 1-3: (K1, P1) to end.

Rnd 4: (SSK, K8, K2tog) twice. (20 sts)

Rnd 5: Knit.

Rnd 6: (SSK, K6, K2tog) twice. (16 sts)

Rnd 7: Knit.

Rnd 8: (SSK, K4, K2tog) twice. (12 sts)

Rnd 9: Knit.

Rnd 10: (SSSK, K3tog) twice. (4 sts)

Break yarn, pull through remaining sts.

Finishing

Tack the tail ends to the body as shown in the photos, sew CO edges together, closing tail.

Stitch the flippers to the walrus body as shown in the photos. Using Color E stitch eyes and nostrils as shown.

Using Color D stitch whiskers.
Using Color C stitch two tusks.

Close top of head using yarn tail. Using Color B stitch the hat on the walrus head.

Weave in ends.
Thread 5" of yarn or ribbon through top, tie together to hang ornament from.

WHALE

Yarn

A Marble Heather 24244; B Pimento 24246; C Asphalt Heather 24243; one skein each

Notes:

The ornament is meant to look two-dimensional. To achieve this effect, stuff only lightly.

Directions

Head

With Color A and smaller needles (used for all sections of the Whale except the Scarf), CO 10 sts. Join to work in the round, PM if desired.

Rnd 1: (KFB, K3, KFB) twice. (14 sts)

Rnd 2: Knit.

Rnd 3: (KFB, K5, KFB) twice. (18 sts)

Rnd 4: Knit.

Rnd 5: (KFB, K7, KFB) twice. (22 sts)

Rnd 6: Knit.

Rnd 7: (KFB, K9, KFB) twice. (26 sts)

Rnd 8: Knit.

Rnd 9: (KFB, K11, KFB) twice. (30 sts)

Rnd 10: Knit.

Rnd 11: (KFB, K13, KFB) twice. (34 sts)

Rnds 12-13: Knit.

Rnd 14: (KFB, K15, KFB) twice. (38 sts)

Rnds 15-17: Knit.

Rnd 18: (KFB, K17, KFB) twice. (42 sts)

Body

Rnds 19-23: Knit.

Rnd 24: (K2tog, K17, SSK) twice. (38 sts)

Rnds 25-28: Knit.

Rnds 29-33: (K2tog, K15, SSK) twice. (34 sts)

Rnd 34: (K2tog, K13, SSK) twice. (30 sts)

Rnds 35-38: Knit.

Rnd 39: K25, W&T; P20, W&T; K15, W&T; P10, W&T; K20, knitting wraps with sts when you come to them.

Rnd 40: (K2tog, K11, SSK) twice. (26 sts)

Rnds 41-43: Knit.

Rnd 44: (K2tog, K9, SSK) twice. (22 sts)

Rnds 45-46: Knit.

Stuff whale here.

Rnd 47: K19, W&T; P16, W&T; K12, W&T; P8, W&T; K15, knitting wraps with sts when you come to them.

Rnd 48: Knit.

Rnd 49: (K2tog, K7, SSK) twice. (18 sts)

Rnd 50: Knit.

Rnd 51: K15, W&T; P12, W&T; K9, W&T; P6, W&T; K12, knitting wraps with sts when you come to them.

Rnd 52: Knit.

Rnd 53: (K2tog, K5, SSK) twice. (14 sts)

Rnd 54: Knit.

Rnd 55: (K2tog, K3, SSK) twice. (10 sts)

Rnd 56: Knit.

Stuff the remaining whale here.

Tail

Rnd 57: K4, turn; Sl 1, P2, turn; Sl 1, K7, turn; Sl 1 P2, turn; Sl 1, K3.

Rnd 58: K2, place next 5 sts on scrap yarn, KFB, K2. (6 sts)

Rnd 59: KFB, K4, KFB. (8 sts)

Rnd 60: Knit.

Rnd 61: KFB, K6, KFB. (10 sts)

Rnd 62: Knit.

Rnd 63: KFB, K8, KFB. (12 sts)

Rnds 64-65: Knit.

Rnd 66: (K2tog, K2, SSK) twice. (8 sts)

Rnd 67: Knit.

Rnd 68: (K2tog, SSK) twice. (4 sts)

Break yarn, pull through remaining sts.

Return held sts to needles. Join yarn on outer edge (whale's belly side).

Set up Rnd: K3, KFB, K2. (6 sts)

Work as previous side of the tail, beginning with Rnd 59.

Flippers (make two)

With Color A, CO 4 sts. Join to work in the round, PM if desired.

Rnd 1: Knit.

Rnd 2: KFB, K2, KFB. (6 sts)

Rnd 3: Knit.

Rnd 4: KFB, K4, KFB. (8 sts)

Rnd 5: Knit.

Rnd 6: KFB, K6, KFB. (10 sts)

Rnd 7: Knit.

Rnd 8: KFB, K8, KFB. (12 sts)

Rnd 9: Knit.

Rnd 10: KFB, K10, KFB. (14 sts)

Rnd 11: Knit.

Rnd 12: KFB, K12, KFB. (16 sts)

Rnd 13: Knit.

Rnd 14: KFB, K14, KFB. (18 sts)

Rnd 15: Knit.

Work a 3-Needle Bind Off. Leave an 8" tail, break yarn.

Scarf

With Color B and larger needles CO 55 sts. Knit 3 rows, bind off.

Finishing

Using the 8" tail, stitch the flippers to the whale body as shown in the photos.

Using Color C, stitch eyes and mouth as shown.
Weave in ends.

Knot scarf in place around whale.
Thread 5" of yarn or ribbon through top, tie together to hang ornament from.

POLAR BEAR
Yarn

A Cream 23730; B Grass 24585; C Green Tea Heather 24258; D Marble Heather 24244; one skein each

Notes:
The ornament is meant to look two-dimensional. To achieve this effect stuff only lightly. Stitching around the arms after stuffing will pucker the body to look like arms. Arm stitching will run along the increase/decrease line between Rnd 10 and Rnd 35. See photos.

Directions
Bottom

With Color A and smaller needles (used for all sections of the Polar Bear), CO 20 sts leaving an 8" tail to stitch up the opening later. Join to work in the round, PM if desired.

Rnd 1: (KFB, K8, KFB) twice. (24 sts)

Rnd 2: (KFB, K10, KFB) twice. (28 sts)

Rnd 3: (KFB, K12, KFB) twice. (32 sts)

Rnd 4: Knit.

Rnd 5: (KFB, K14, KFB) twice. (36 sts)

Rnd 6: Knit.

Rnd 7: (KFB, K16, KFB) twice. (40 sts)

Rnds 8-9: Knit.

Rnd 10: (KFB, K18, KFB) twice. (44 sts)

Rnd 11: (KFB, K1, KFB, K16, KFB, K1, KFB) twice. (52 sts)

Rnd 12: (KFB, K2, KFB, K18, KFB, K2, KFB) twice. (60 sts)

Rnd 13: Knit.

Rnd 14: (KFB, K28, KFB) twice. (64 sts)

Rnds 15-16: Knit.

Break Color A. Join Color B.

Sweater

Rnd 17: Knit.

Rnds 18-20: Purl.

Join and begin working in Color C.

Rnds 21-22: Knit.

Rnd 23: (K6, K2tog, K16, SSK, K6) twice. (60 sts)

Change to Color B.

Rnds 24-25: Knit.

Rnd 26: (K5, K2tog, K16, SSK, K5) twice. (56 sts)

Change to Color C.

Rnds 27-28: Knit.

Rnd 29: (K5, K2tog, K14, SSK, K5) twice. (52 sts)

Change to Color B.

Rnds 30-31: Knit.

Rnd 32: (K5, K2tog, K12, SSK, K5) twice. (48 sts)

Change to Color C.

Rnds 33-34: Knit.

Rnd 35: (K5, K2tog, K10, SSK, k5) twice. (44 sts)

Change to Color B.

Rnds 36-37: Knit.

Rnd 38: (K2tog, K18, SSK) twice. (40 sts)

Change to Color C.

Rnd 39: Knit.

Rnd 40: (K2tog, K16, SSK) twice. (36 sts)

Rnd 41: (K2tog, K14, SSK) twice. (32 sts)

Break Color C.

Collar
Work with Color B.
Rnd 42: Knit.
Rnds 43-45: (K1, P1) to end.
Rnd 46: Purl.
Break Color C, join Color A.

Head
Rnd 47: (K2tog, K12, SSK) twice. (28 sts)
Rnds 48-53: Knit.
Rnd 54: (KFB, K12, KFB) twice. (32 sts)
Rnds 55-56: Knit.
Rnd 45: (K2tog, K12, SSK) twice. (28 sts)
Rnd 46: Knit.
Rnd 47: (K2tog, K10, SSK) twice. (24 sts)
Rnd 48: Knit.
Rnd 49: (K2tog, K8, SSK) twice. (20 sts)
Break yarn, graft front 10 sts with the back 10 sts.

Ears (make two)
With Color A, CO 6 sts. Join to work in the round, PM if desired.
Rnd 1: (KFB, K1, KFB) twice. (10 sts)
Rnd 2-4: Knit.

Work a 3-Needle Bind Off. Break yarn, leaving an 8" tail for joining to body.

Finishing
Using the opening at the bottom, stuff the bear with fiberfill. Graft together the two sides of the bottom edge using the CO tail.

Using the long tails, stitch the ears to the body as shown.
Weave in ends.

Using Color D stitch eyes and nose as shown.

Using Color D and starting at the decrease of Rnd 35, work a running stitch down along the increases. Stitch around hand, then back up to the armpit. See photos.

Thread 5" of yarn or ribbon through top, tie together to hang ornament from.

Annie Watts has tried every craft under the sun and is happy to have finally rooted her talents in the knitting world. As a Colorado native, she is happy to have a home with such crazy weather that handknit wool sweaters can still be worn in June and cotton socks in December. She tries to keep wool and needles in her hands as much as humanly possible.

MINI-MITTS

by SpillyJane

FINISHED MEASUREMENTS
4.5" high x 3.5" circumference

YARN
Knit Picks Palette (100% Peruvian Highland Wool; 231 yards/50g): A Serpentine 25100, B Lipstick 24245, C White 23728, D Tranquil 25094, E Cosmopolitan 24568, F Abyss Heather 25993; 1 ball each.

NEEDLES
US 0 (2mm) set of 5 DPNs, or size to obtain gauge

NOTIONS
Yarn Needle
8" length of Scrap Yarn

GAUGE
44 sts and 44 rows = 4" in stranded St st in the round, blocked.

Mini-Mitts

Notes:

These four matching miniscule mittens are sure to add a little knitted magic to your holiday tree. SpillyJane's classic Swedish Fish, Gnomes, and Wintertime for Adriana mittens have been shrunk down to ornament size and paired with the new Volute design. Knit one, knit them all, or mix and match.

Each of these mitts is a miniature replica of a full-sized SpillyJane-style mitten with its own tiny, but properly executed Peasant thumb. These are a great way to practice colourwork on a small scale before you commit to making a full-sized pair!

The mini mittens are worked from cuff to tip. As these mittens are ornaments and not intended to be worn, only instructions for the left-hand mitten are provided. There are four different mini mittens to make; choose a pattern and work accordingly.
One ball of each of the six coordinating colorways of Knit Picks Palette will provide you with a multitude of miniature mittens.

I-Cord
*Knit a row. Slide row to other end of needle without turning work. Pull yarn firmly and repeat from *, creating a tube.

2x2 Ribbing
All Rounds: (K2 TBL, P2) to end.

DIRECTIONS
Cuff
Using the Row 1 color of the chosen chart (Gnomes, Swedish Fish, Wintertime for Adriana or Volute) loosely CO 40 sts. Arrange sts across 4 dpns so that there are 10 sts on each. Each needle will now be known respectively as Needle 1, 2, 3, or 4.
Work 8 rounds of 2x2 Ribbing.
The Cuff is now complete.

Body of Mitten
Begin to work from the chosen chart, beginning with Round 1 and working right to left until Round 16 where there is an outline for thumb placement.

Thumb Placement Round
Rnd 16: Work Round 16 across Needles 1, 2, 3 and 4 until outline denoting thumb placement. Drop working yarn. Knit the next 5 sts using the piece of scrap yarn. Slide the 5 sts that were just knit with the scrap yarn back onto the right-hand needle. Drop scrap yarn and take up working yarn again. Continue working in pattern as per chosen chart across the scrap yarn-worked sts to the end of round. The thumb placement round is now complete.

Continue working from chosen chart until Round 33 where the mitten tip decreases begin.

Mitten Tip Decreases
Decrease for Mitten tips as follows:
Needle 1: SL 1, K1, PSSO; continue to work as per pattern.
Needle 2: Work as per patt until 2 sts remain; K2tog.
Needle 3: Repeat as for Needle 1.
Needle 4: Repeat as for Needle 2. 4 sts dec per round, 1 on each needle.

Repeat this procedure across each round until 4 sts remain, working the final round to the end of Needle 4. There should now be 1 st on each needle. Break yarn, leaving a generous tail. Use yarn needle to draw yarn tail through 4 remaining live sts to close top of mini mitten. Prepare to knit thumb.

Thumb
The thumb of the Mini Mitten is worked in the same colour as the mitten's cuff. PU 5 sts both above and below the sts held on the scrap yarn for a total of 10 sts, discarding the scrap yarn when finished. Divide the sts evenly across three needles and prepare to begin working in the round.

Work thumb in St st in the round for a total of 12 rounds.

Thumb Tip Decreases
Decrease for thumb tip as follows:
Needle 1: SL 1, K1, PSSO; continue to work as per pattern.
Needle 2: Work as per pattern until 2 sts remain; K2tog.
Needle 3: Repeat as for Needle 1.
Needle 4: Repeat as for Needle 2. 6 sts rem.

Divide the 6 sts across 2 needles, with 3 sts on each. Now, proceed as follows:
Needle 1: SL 2 sts Kwise, K next st, pass 2 slipped sts over.
Needle 2: Repeat procedure described as per needle 1. 2 sts dec on each needle, 2 sts rem.

Break yarn and draw through both live sts to close top of thumb. Draw tail into the inside of thumb and weave in all ends.

I-cord for Hanging
CO 3 stitches. Work I-cord over 3 sts for 5"(10cm) or until desired length. Bind off. Fold finished I-cord in half and attach either end together to form a loop and then stitch to top of mitten (or corner of cuff) for hanging on a holiday tree or wherever you like.

Finishing
Weave in ends, press or steam lightly with an iron if desired.

Legend

Symbol	Name	Description
☐ (white)	knit	knit stitch
■ (grey)	No Stitch	Placeholder - No stitch made.
λ	sl1 k psso	slip 1, knit 1, pass slipped stitch over knit 1
╱	k2tog	Knit two stitches together as one stitch
■ (brown)	A Serpentine	
■ (red)	B Lipstick	
☐ (white)	C White	
■ (green)	D Tranquil	
■ (coral)	E Cosmopolitan	
■ (black)	F Abyss Heather	

Gnomes Chart

Volute Chart

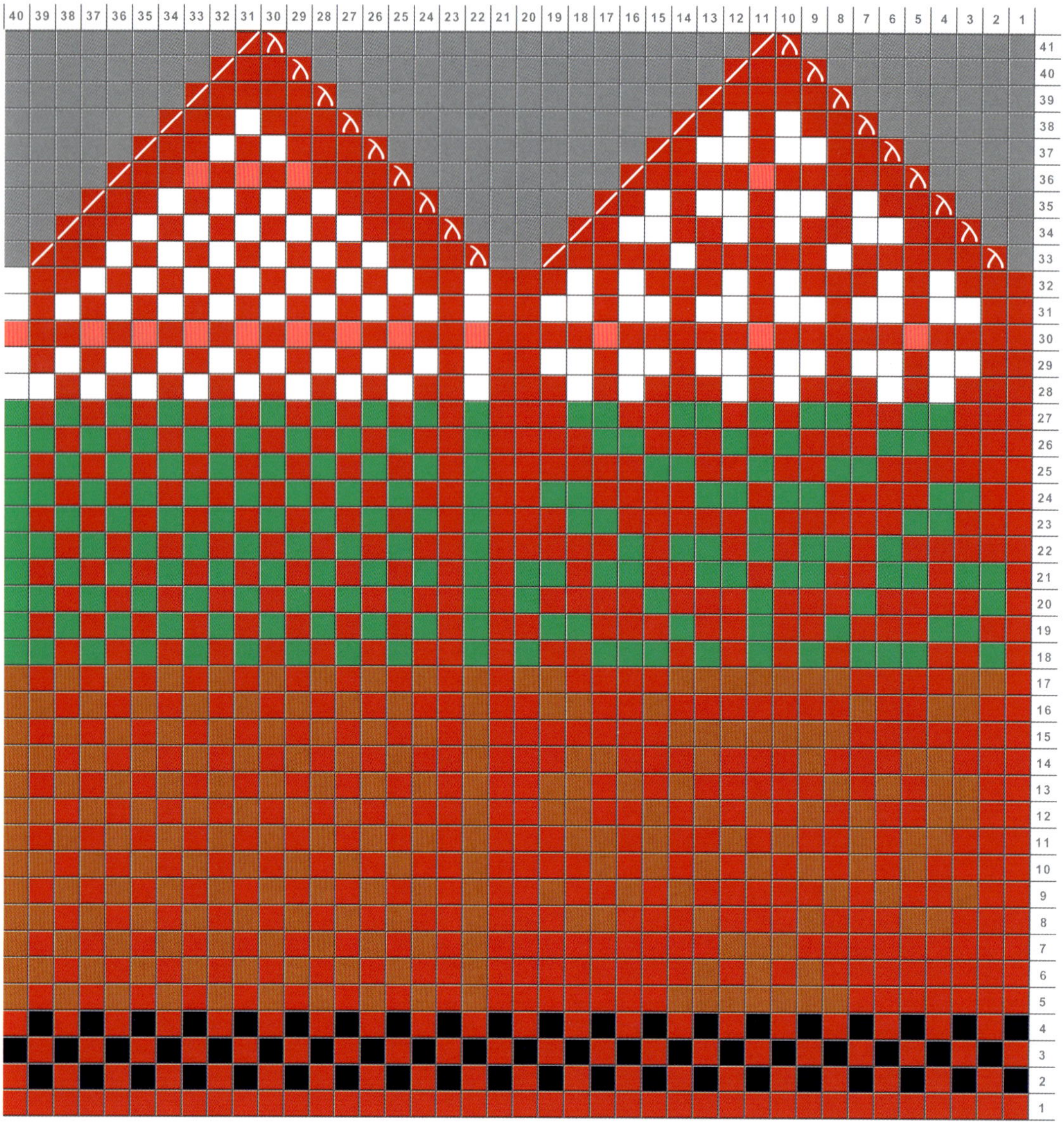

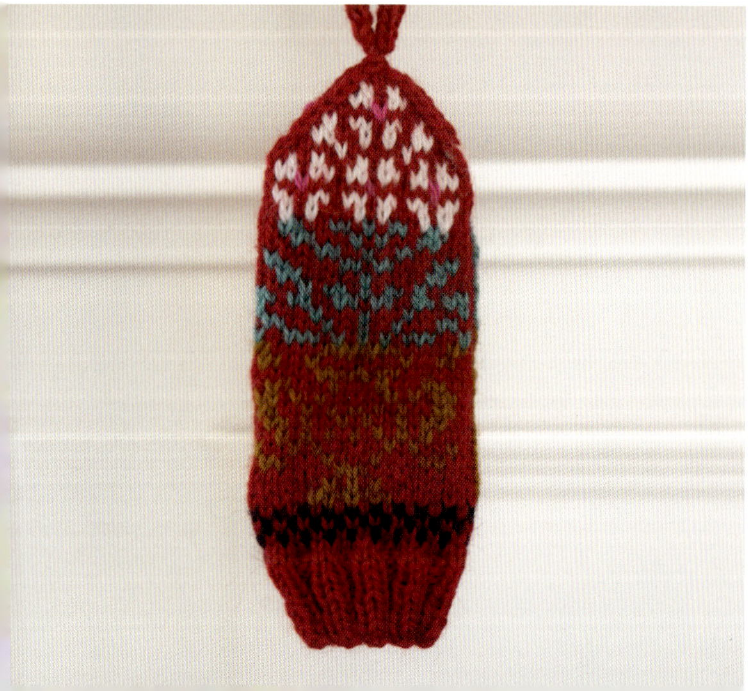

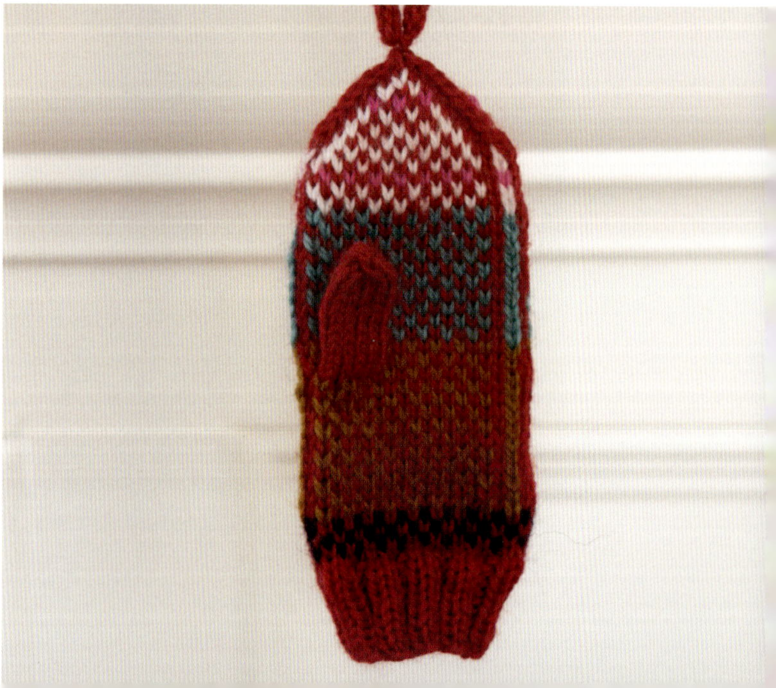

Swedish Fish Chart

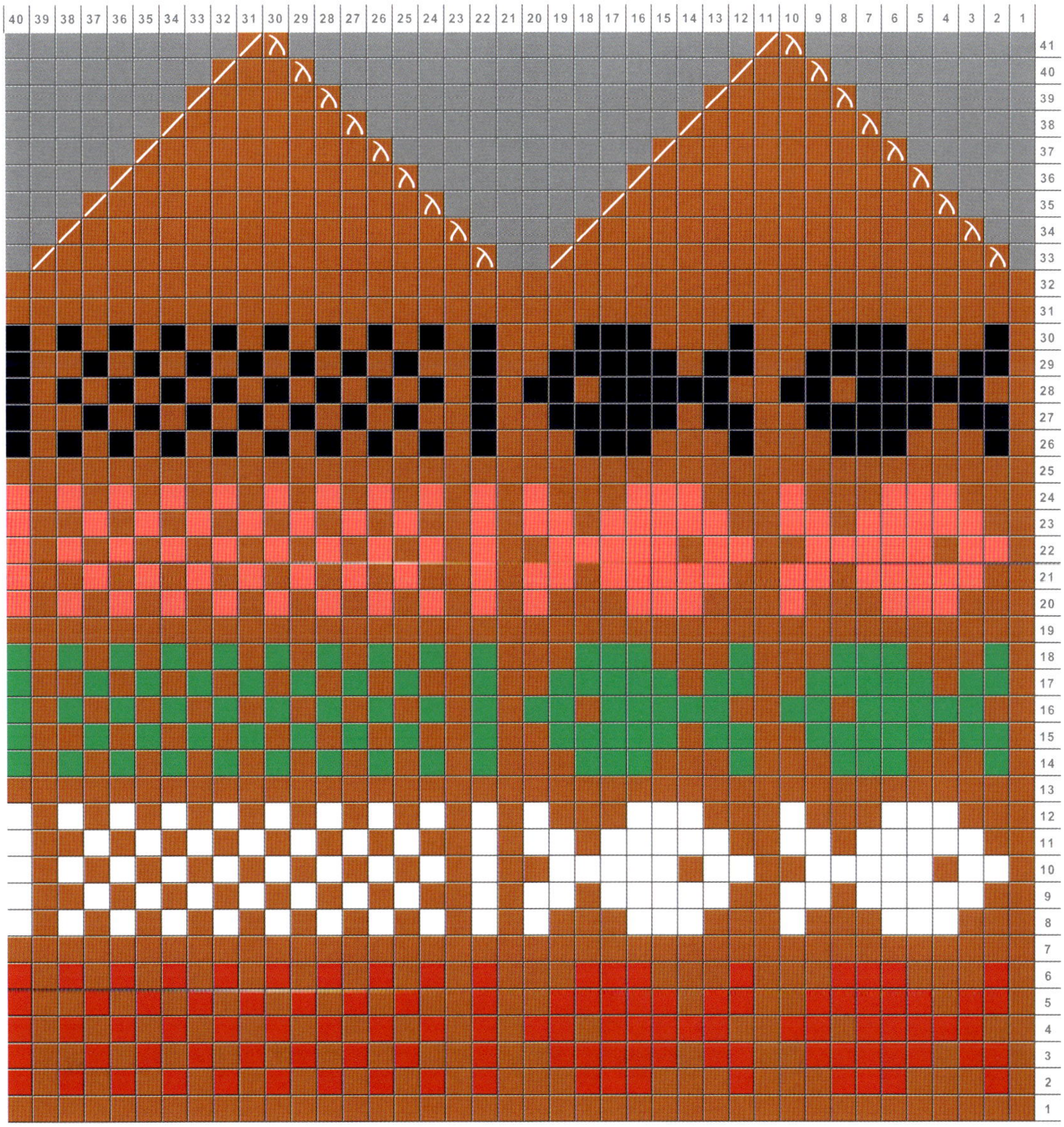

Winter Chart

SpillyJane is a knitter/designer, writer, and weirdo from Windsor, Ontario, Canada. She lives in a 100 year old house with her husband David and her avian companion Earl. She really, really likes mittens. See more of her adventures in knitting (and more!) at spillyjane.blogspot.com.

ICY SEAS

by Hunter Hammersen

FINISHED MEASUREMENTS

Approximately 7" circumference x 3.25" in height.

YARN

Knit Picks Bare Gloss Fingering 23998 (70% Merino Wool, 30% Silk; 440 yards/100g): 1 hank to easily make all 4 ornaments with plenty to spare for extras. Each of these hats took about 7 grams or 30 yards of yarn

NEEDLES

US 1.5 (2.5mm) DPNs or circular needles, or size to obtain gauge.

NOTIONS

Yarn Needle
Stitch Markers
Cable Needle

GAUGE

32 sts and 42 Rows = 4" in 1 x 1 Twisted Ribbing, blocked.

Icy Seas

Notes: Each hat features delightfully intricate twisted stitch cables. These can look a bit intimidating, but they're really not hard (and are well worth the effort). Plus, this is a perfect place to practice them before moving on to a larger project.

Be sure to work the stitches as true cables, not the 'left twist' or 'right twist' technique you may see described elsewhere. Working them as true cables ensures better stitch definition. It's fine to cable without a cable needle, but do be sure you're working true cables.

When working the charts and knitting in the round, read each row from right to left. When working flat, read RS Rows (odd numbers) from right to left, and WS Rows (even numbers) from left to right.

If you like the fabric you're getting, let that be your guide more than matching exact gauge. These are quite forgiving, and the size is quite flexible. They'll still be cute if they're a bit bigger or smaller!

1 x 1 Cable, Right Twisted
SL 1 to CN, hold in back, KTBL, KTBL from CN.

1 x 1 Cable, Left Twisted
SL 1 to CN, hold in front, KTBL, KTBL from CN.

1 x 1 Cable, Right Twisted over Purl
SL 1 to CN, hold in back, KTBL, purl 1 from CN.

1 x 1 Cable, Left Twisted over Purl
SL 1 to CN, hold in front, purl 1, KTBL from CN.

Right-leaning Twisted Knit Decrease
SL 1 as if to purl. Remount the next stitch so it is rotated 180 degrees (one half turn) clockwise. Return the slipped stitch to the left needle. K2TOG.

Left-leaning Twisted Knit Decrease
Insert the right needle from the right to the left into the back loops of 2 sts. Knit both together.

Right-leaning Twisted Purl Decrease
SL 1 as if to purl. Remount the next stitch so it is rotated 180 degrees (one half turn) clockwise. Return the slipped stitch to the left needle. P2TOG.

Left-leaning Twisted Purl Decrease
P2TOGTBL.

FRAZIL
When ocean water begins to freeze, it creates small, needle-like crystals called frazil.

Directions
Brim, Body, & Decreases
CO 48 sts. PM and join for working in the round.
Work Rows 1-7 of the Frazil chart three times. Work Rows 8-16 once. 6 sts remain.

Cut yarn leaving an 8" tail. Using a yarn needle, thread the tail through the remaining 6 sts and draw tight.

Continue to Finishing.

NILAS
As the water continues to freeze, if the water is calm, frazil crystals come together to form thin, elastic sheets of ice called nilas.

Directions
Brim
CO 48 sts. PM and join for working in the round.

Ribbing Rnd: *P1 TBL, K1 TBL, P1 TBL; rep from * around.

Work 18 total rounds of this ribbing. (Note, you're working your purls through the back loop so that, when you turn the brim of the hat up, you'll see twisted stitches. You can switch to regular purl stitches when you get to the chart.)

Body & Decreases
Work the Nilas chart once. 4 sts remain.

Cut yarn leaving an 8" tail. Using a yarn needle, thread the tail through the remaining 4 sts and draw tight.

Continue to Finishing.

SHUGA
If it's windy or the water is choppy while the ice is forming, it can shape itself into small, spongy lumps called shuga.

Directions
Brim
CO 50 sts. PM and join for working in the round.

Work Rows 1-8 of the Shuga chart once.

Body
Work Rows 9-12 of the Shuga chart 4 times.

Decreases
Work Rows 13-22 of the appropriate chart once. 8 stitches remain.

Cut yarn leaving an 8" tail. Using a yarn needle, thread the tail through the remaining 8 sts and draw tight.

Continue to Finishing.

BRECCIA
When pieces of ice at different stages of development freeze together, the combination is called breccia ice.

Directions
Brim
The brim of this hat is worked flat. Then, stitches are picked up along one side of the flat piece, joined to work in the round, and the body of the hat knit upward.

CO 12 sts (leave a tail of about a foot). Work Rows 1-12 of the Breccia chart 7 times. Work Rows 13-23 once. BO 2 remaining sts.

Take a moment now to block the brim, being sure to keep the edges straight and even. This will make it easier to pick up stitches in the next step.

Body
Hold the brim so that the narrow edge is at the bottom, the point

is at the top, and the right side of the knitting is facing you. Find the column of slipped stitches along the leftmost edge of the piece (these were column 12 on the chart).

Using a circular needle or 2 DPNs, pick up the back leg of each slipped stitch. Only pick up stitches on the straight part, not the part that narrows to a point. You should pick up a total of 45 stitches.

PM and join for working in the round (so the right side of the brim piece is facing out).

Knit every stitch of every row for 24 rounds.

Decreases
Dec Rnd 1: (SSK, K3) 9 times. 36 sts remain.
Dec Rnd 2: (SSK, K2) 9 times. 27 sts remain.
Dec Rnd 3: (SSK, K1) 9 times. 18 sts remain.
Dec Rnd 4: SSK 9 times. 9 sts remain.

Cut yarn leaving an 8" tail. Using a yarn needle, thread the tail through the remaining 6 sts and draw tight.

Continue to Finishing.

Finishing
Weave in ends. Block vigorously. You can use anything round and the right size (like a lightbulb, a plastic easter egg, a darning egg, or a tennis ball). Look around, you've almost certainly got something on hand you can use!

Individual Finishing Notes:

For Breccia, use the tail you left when you cast on to tack down the point of the brim when you weave in your ends.

For Nilas, fold up the brim before blocking (it may help to pin it in place to keep it straight while it dries).

For Shuga, put the hat over whatever you're using to block it then grab the tip and pull it up a bit to emphasize the point at the top of the hat.

Legend

slip
RS: Slip stitch as if to purl, holding yarn in back
WS: Slip stitch as if to purl, holding yarn in front

purl
RS: purl stitch
WS: knit stitch

knit tbl
RS: Knit stitch through back loop
WS: Purl stitch through back loop

knit
RS: knit stitch
WS: purl stitch

1 x 1 cable, left twisted over purl
SL 1 to CN, hold in front, purl 1, KTBL from CN

1 x 1 cable, left twisted
SL 1 to CN, hold in front, purl 1, KTBL from CN

1 x 1 cable, right twisted
SL 1 to CN, hold in back, KTBL, KTBL from CN

1 x 1 cable, right twisted over purl
SL 1 to CN, hold in back, KTBL, purl 1 from CN

No Stitch
Placeholder - No stitch made.

Left-leaning twisted decrease
RS: Insert the right needle from the right to the left into the back loops of 2 sts. Knit both together
WS: P2TOGTBL

Right-leaning twisted decrease
RS: SL 1 as if to purl. Remount the next stitch so it is rotated 180 degrees (one half turn) clockwise. Return the slipped stitch to the left needle. K2TOG

WS: SL 1 as if to purl. Remount the next stitch so it is rotated 180 degrees (one half turn) clockwise. Return the slipped stitch to the left needle. P2TOG

Frazil Chart

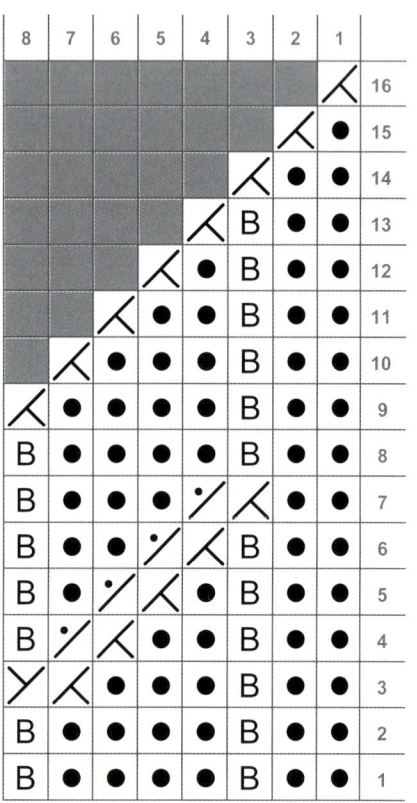

8	7	6	5	4	3	2	1	
							⋏	16
						⋏	●	15
					⋏	●	●	14
				⋏	B	●	●	13
			⋏	●	B	●	●	12
		⋏	●	●	B	●	●	11
	⋏	●	●	●	B	●	●	10
⋏	●	●	●	●	B	●	●	9
B	●	●	●	●	B	●	●	8
B	●	●	⋰	⋏	B	●	●	7
B	●	●	⋰	⋏	B	●	●	6
B	●	⋰	⋏	●	B	●	●	5
B	⋰	⋏	●	●	B	●	●	4
⋎	⋏	●	●	●	B	●	●	3
B	●	●	●	●	B	●	●	2
B	●	●	●	●	B	●	●	1

Nilas Chart

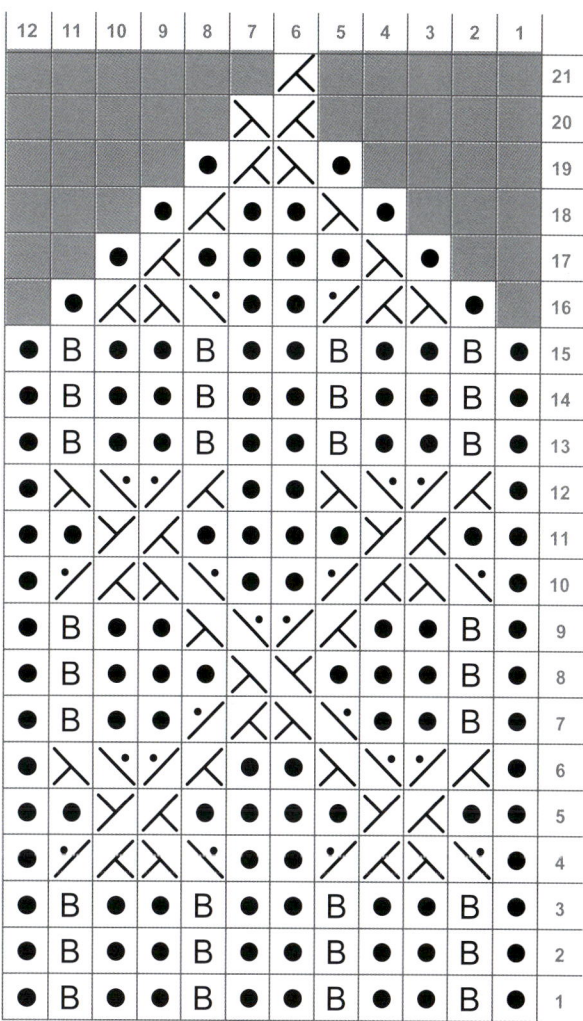

Shuga Chart

Columns (left to right): 25, 24, 23, 22, 21, 20, 19, 18, 17, 16, 15, 14, 13, 12, 11, 10, 9, 8, 7, 6, 5, 4, 3, 2, 1

Rows (bottom to top): 1 through 22

Breccia Chart

12	11	10	9	8	7	6	5	4	3	2	1	Row
░	░	░	░	╳	╳	░	░	░	░	░	░	23
░	░	░	░	╳	╳	░	░	░	░	░	░	22
░	░	░	V	●	╳	╳	●	V	░	░	░	21
░	░	░	●	●	╱╲	╱╲	●	●	░	░	░	20
░	V	●	●	╱╲	╱╲	╱╲	●	●	V	░	░	19
V	●	●	B	●	B	B	●	B	●	●		18
	●	●	B	●	B	B	●	B	●	●	V	17
V	●	●	B	●	B	B	●	B	●	●		16
	●	●	B	●	B	B	●	B	●	●	V	15
V	●	●	B	●	B	B	●	B	●	●		14
	●	●	B	●	B	B	●	B	●	●	V	13
V	●	●	B	●	B	B	●	B	●	●		12
	●	●	╲	╲·	╱	╱	╲·	╱	●	●	V	11
V	●	●	●	B	B	B	B	●	●	●		10
	●	●	●	╱	╱╲	╱╲	╱	●	●	●	V	9
V	●	●	●	B	B	B	B	●	●	●		8
	●	●	╱	╲	╱╲	╱╲	╲	·	●	●	V	7
V	●	●	B	●	B	B	●	B	●	●		6
	●	●	B	●	B	B	●	B	●	●	V	5
V	●	●	B	●	B	B	●	B	●	●		4
	●	●	B	●	B	B	●	B	●	●	V	3
V	●	●	B	●	B	B	●	B	●	●		2
	●	●	B	●	B	B	●	B	●	●	V	1

Hunter Hammersen didn't really like knitting the first time she tried it. She didn't much care for it the second time either. It wasn't till the third time, and the discovery of knitted socks, that she was properly smitten. Once she realized she could make up her own patterns, her fate was sealed. She's been busy designing ever since.

You can follow her adventures at www.violentlydomestic.com.

Abbreviations			M	marker			stitch		TBL	through back loop
BO	bind off		M1	make one stitch		RH	right hand		TFL	through front loop
cn	cable needle		M1L	make one left-leaning		rnd(s)	round(s)		tog	together
CC	contrast color			stitch		RS	right side		W&T	wrap & turn (see
CDD	Centered double dec		M1R	make one right-lean-		Sk	skip			specific instructions
CO	cast on			ing stitch		Sk2p	sl 1, k2tog, pass			in pattern)
cont	continue		MC	main color			slipped stitch over		WE	work even
dec	decrease(es)		P	purl			k2tog: 2 sts dec		WS	wrong side
DPN(s)	double pointed		P2tog	purl 2 sts together		SKP	sl, k, psso: 1 st dec		WYIB	with yarn in back
	needle(s)		PM	place marker		SL	slip		WYIF	with yarn in front
EOR	every other row		PFB	purl into the front and		SM	slip marker		YO	yarn over
inc	increase			back of stitch		SSK	sl, sl, k these 2 sts tog			
K	knit		PSSO	pass slipped stitch		SSP	sl, sl, p these 2 sts tog			
K2tog	knit two sts together			over			tbl			
KFB	knit into the front and		PU	pick up		SSSK	sl, sl, sl, k these 3 sts			
	back of stitch		P wise	purlwise			tog			
K-wise	knitwise		rep	repeat		St st	stockinette stitch			
LH	left hand		Rev St st	reverse stockinette		sts	stitch(es)			

Knit Picks yarn is both luxe and affordable—a seeming contradiction trounced! But it's not just about the pretty colors; we also care deeply about fiber quality and fair labor practices, leaving you with a gorgeously reliable product you'll turn to time and time again.

THIS COLLECTION FEATURES

Palette
Fingering Weight
100% Peruvian Highland Wool

Gloss Fingering
Fingering Weight
70% Merino Wool, 30% Silk

Wool of the Andes
Worsted Weight
100% Peruvian Highland Wool

View these beautiful yarns and more at www.KnitPicks.com